DATE DUE

NOV 2 0 1985				
FEB 2 3 1993				
AUG 1 6 1993				
JUN 1 0 1994				
NOV 2 2 1999				
MAY 5 2000				
OCT 3 0 2000				
NOV 2 3 2004				

NORTH AND SOUTH KOREA

← A FIRST BOOK →

BY GENE AND CLARE GURNEY

NORTH & SOUTH KOREA

FRANKLIN WATTS, INC.
NEW YORK | 1973

*Frontispiece, large stone Buddhas like this
one are found everywhere in Korea.*

Cover by One + One Studio
Map by George Buctel

Photographs courtesy of:
Charles Phelps Cushing: p. 13; Embassy of Japan:
frontispiece, p. 2; Korean Research and Information Office: pp. 5 (top and bottom), 10, 29, 32, 59,
65; U.S. Army: pp. 15, 19, 22 (top and bottom), 24,
30 (top and bottom), 35 (top and bottom), 38, 40
43, 47, 50, 54, 56, 60, 69, 72, 80, 81, 82

Library of Congress Cataloging in Publication Data

Gurney, Gene.
   North and South Korea.

   (A First book)
   SUMMARY: Discusses the geography, history,
industries, customs, and cities of a country divided
by war and political philosophy.
   Bibliography: p.
   1. Korea–Juvenile literature. [1. Korea] I. Gurney, Clare, joint author. II. Title.
DS902.G87   915.19   73-4278
ISBN 0-531-00804-5

TABLE OF CONTENTS

NORTH AND SOUTH KOREA

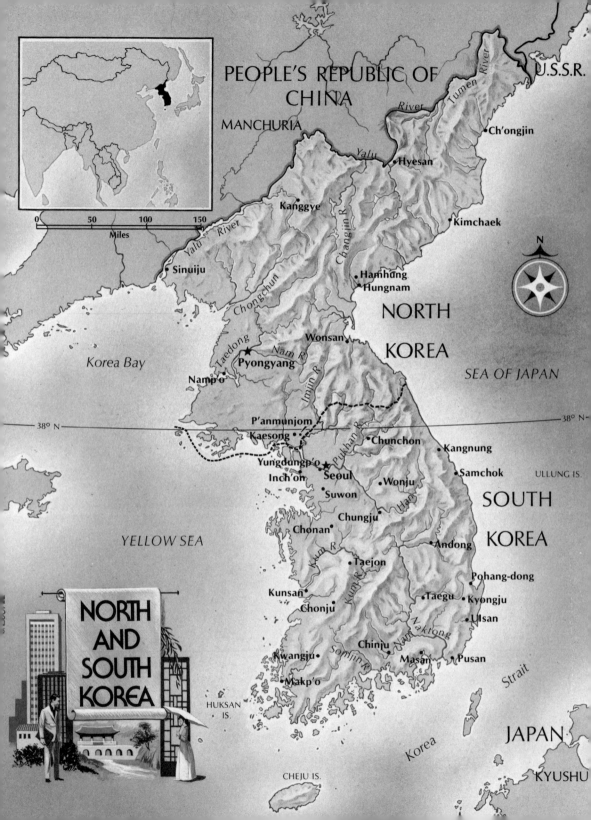

PEOPLE'S REPUBLIC OF CHINA

MANCHURIA

U.S.S.R.

Tumen River

River

Yalu

Ch'ongjin

Hyesan

Kanggye

Kimchaek

Yalu River

Changjin R.

Sinuiju

Hamhŭng

Hungnam

Chongchun

Taedong

Wonsan

NORTH

KOREA

Korea Bay

Nam R.

Pyongyang

SEA OF JAPAN

Namp'o

Imjin R.

38° N

38° N

P'anmunjom

Kaesong

Chunchon

Kangnung

Yungdŭngp'o

Pukhan R.

Inch'on

Seoul

Samchok

ULLUNG IS.

Suwon

Wonju

SOUTH

Chungju

Han R.

KOREA

Chonan

Kum R.

Andong

YELLOW SEA

Taejon

Pohang-dong

Kunsan

Taegu

Kyongju

Chonju

Naktong R.

Ulsan

Chinju

Nam R.

Kwangju

Somjin R.

Masan

Pusan

Makp'o

Strait

HUKSAN IS.

Korea

JAPAN

CHEJU IS.

KYUSHU

N

NORTH AND SOUTH KOREA

0   50   100   150
Miles

1

KOREA, AN ANCIENT
AND BEAUTIFUL COUNTRY

Korea is one of the oldest countries in the world. People were living in what is now Korea long before there were historians to write about them. A favorite Korean legend traces the country's beginnings to Hwanung, the son of the Heavenly Ruler. Hwanung came to earth and fell in love with a beautiful young woman who had been changed from a bear into a human being. Their son, Tan'gun, became the first king of Korea in 2333 B.C. Tan'gun, according to the legend, ruled for 1,200 years and taught his subjects agriculture and other accomplishments.

During its long history, Korea has had several names. One of the oldest is Choson, or Land of the Morning Calm, a name that fits the country's natural beauty. The name Korea, which means high and beautiful, also describes the country because Korea is a land of scenic mountains, blue skies, and crystal-clear streams.

On the north, the rugged Korean peninsula borders on Siberia, the eastern part of the Soviet Union, and on the region in northeastern China known as Manchuria. Korea extends southeastward to within 120 miles of the main Japanese islands of Honshu and Kyushu. The peninsula is separated from Siberia by the Tumen River and from Manchuria by the Yalu River. The Sea of Japan and the Korea Strait separate Korea from Japan. On the west, the Yellow Sea lies between Korea and the People's Republic of China.

The Korean peninsula is approximately 525 miles long and from 125 to 200 miles wide. Its 85,000-square-mile area is about equal to the size of the state of Utah. Many islands dot the peninsula's 6,000 miles of coastline, most of them along the south and west coasts.

Although Korea is a mountainous country, only one peak, Kaektu Mountain in the extreme north, is higher than 9,000 feet. The mountain ranges that run almost the full length of the east coast rise steeply from the sea. Small but fertile lowlands are found in western, central, and southern Korea where rivers have deposited rich soils. It is in these lowlands that most Koreans live.

Korea has many rivers, but few are important to navigation because they are swift and shallow with numerous sandbars and rapids. The major rivers are the Naktong which flows through southeast Korea, the Han in the center of the peninsula, the Taedong in the north, and the Yalu on the northwestern border. There are also a few lakes in Korea, all very small.

On the west, Korea's coast is honeycombed with thousands of bays and dotted with numerous small islands. Here the difference between high tide and low tide may be as much as thirty feet. Such extreme tides make navigation difficult.

Korea's climate is similar in many respects to that of the region between Maine and Georgia in the United States. In winter, Korea lies in the path of cold, dry air moving outward from central Asia. In the north, temperatures are below freezing. In the south, however, winter temperatures are influenced by the warm Kuro Siwo current, the Pacific Ocean equivalent of the Gulf Stream in the Atlantic. Consequently, winters are neither as cold nor as dry as they are in the north.

Summers are hot and moist throughout Korea. The average August temperature exceeds seventy-five degrees Fahrenheit. June, July, and August, the months of the monsoon season, have the heaviest rainfall.

Mountains are the main feature of Korea's terrain.
Rice paddies are in the foreground.

(3)

2

THE KOREAN PEOPLE

The very early ancestors of the present Koreans are believed to have come from Manchuria or northern China nearly three thousand years before the birth of Christ. They were hunters who also fished and gathered berries for food. The Chinese had already learned how to cultivate grain and the migrants may have brought that knowledge with them. The first Korean houses, for winter use, were probably no more than holes in the ground covered with sod roofs.

Today, the typical Korean resembles his northern Chinese neighbors in some ways. Like them, he has dark, straight hair and high cheekbones. But he is apt to be shorter and his jaw protrudes a little more. There is also a resemblance between Koreans and the Japanese, their neighbors to the southeast. Korean men are usually taller than Japanese men, however. Korean women are small in stature, like most Asian women.

Koreans have always had a strong feeling of national identity. Perhaps this is because almost all the inhabitants of the peninsula are of Korean stock. Moreover, for centuries Koreans have used the same language throughout their country. The language belongs to the

Above, Korean village elders in traditional white garb with tall hats of horsehair and silk. Below, two Korean girls in their best gowns for the Day of the Swings festival.

자장은 「다부분의 의견이 한법
부 칙 제 1 조단서의 「이헌법에
의한 대통령, 국회의원선거 기
탈준비는 이헌법시행전에 할
수이쌌다는 규정은 「하지않아
도된다 는 임의규정은 아니며 다
만 기저이헌법이 발효되기전에
선거법을 마련할수이쌌는 법적
근거를 세시히 준거이라고 히석

same group as Mongol, Manchu, Turkic, and Japanese, although spoken Korean is unlike the other languages in the group.

For many centuries, Chinese was the classical language used by Korean scholars, much as European scholars once used Greek and Latin. During the late seventh century, the Koreans developed their own system of writing by adapting Chinese characters to the spoken Korean language. The script, called *idu,* remained in use until the fifteenth century when it was replaced by *han'gul,* the writing system of twenty-four characters that Koreans use today. Scholarly publications continue to employ many Chinese characters, however.

Family ties are strong in Korea. Koreans feel a deep sense of responsibility for others in their family and they willingly make sacrifices to help family members. The traditional Korean family is large. It includes grandparents, parents, sons, daughters-in-law, and their children. When a Korean girl marries, she leaves her own family and becomes a part of her husband's family. Today, however, some Korean families, especially in the cities, are becoming more like American families. They consist of parents and children only.

A Korean father is the head of his family unit and his authority is unquestioned. When the father dies, the oldest son becomes the head of the household. Sons learn from childhood that their first duty is to the family. All children are taught to show respect for parents, grandparents, and older relatives. And they are expected to conduct themselves so that no disgrace will come to their families.

Kim, Yi, and Pak are common family names in Korea just as Jones and Smith are in the United States. Traditionally, a Korean family name comes first, followed by the given name. Instead of saying, "My name is John Smith," a Korean would say, "My name is Smith John." Some Koreans now give their family names last, however, as westerners do.

A sample passage of Korean script in typical box form.
The Korean alphabet contains only 24 characters.

3

THREE THOUSAND YEARS
OF HISTORY

The Koreans began to record their history during the first century
B.C. We know something of what happened before then from ancient ruins and artifacts that have been discovered in various parts
of the peninsula. Stories passed down from father to son also provide information about the early Koreans.

In 1122 B.C., a Chinese government official and scholar named
Kija decided to leave China rather than serve a new emperor. With
about five thousand followers, he left his native country and traveled
south. Korean historians believe that Kija may have settled at Pyongyang in the northwestern part of the peninsula. In Kija's day, the
Koreans were scattered among the river valleys. The people in one
valley had little or no contact with those living in another valley.
Without doing any fighting, Kija was able to establish a kingdom in
northern Korea. He made Pyongyang its capital.

Scholars, artists, and craftsmen came to Korea with Kija. He also
brought experts in agriculture, medicine, and the manufacture of
textiles, all of which were highly developed in China. The raising of
rice and barley began in Korea at this time. Kija himself is said to
have developed a code of laws for his kingdom and he encouraged
the use of the Chinese system of writing. He is also said to have been
responsible for the distinctive broadbrimmed hat traditionally worn

by Korean men. According to one legend, Kija thought the people did too much fighting among themselves. He reasoned that if they were wearing large, expensive hats, they would not risk ruining them in a fight.

During the nearly one thousand years that Kija's dynasty, or family, ruled, the arts and sciences flourished in the kingdom. It was at this time that Korea was first called Choson, or Land of the Morning Calm.

In 193 B.C., a Chinese warrior named Wiman conquered the kingdom founded by Kija. The last ruler of the Kija dynasty barely managed to escape by sea, taking his treasure and some of his followers with him. Wiman quickly won the support of many of the Korean tribes and established a strong government at Pyongyang. However, his grandson, Ugu, was not able to hold out against the Chinese armies that attacked Pyongyang in 108 B.C. After they defeated Ugu, the Chinese divided northern Korea into four colonies.

Meanwhile, southern Korea remained outside Chinese control, although the people there were influenced by Chinese culture. In 57 B.C., the Koreans in the southeastern part of the peninsula established the kingdom of Silla. Another powerful kingdom, called Koguryo, was formed in 37 B.C. in northern Korea where the Chinese rulers had grown weak. A third kingdom, Paekche in southwest Korea, was established in 18 B.C.

During the following seven hundred years, known in Korean history as the Period of the Three Kingdoms, Silla, Koguryo, and Paekche fought each other constantly. Finally, about the middle of the seventh century, Silla became strong enough to conquer the other two kingdoms and unify the peninsula.

Because the Silla rulers of Korea were careful to remain on good terms with China, the country enjoyed many years of peace. Art, literature, and science flourished. It was at this time that people all over the peninsula began to speak the same language.

(9)

Silla kings ruled the Korean peninsula until 935. Then Wang Kon, a powerful general, overthrew the last Silla monarch. He renamed the kingdom Koryo, from which the name Korea comes.

In 1231, Koryo was invaded by fierce tribesmen from Mongolia. To escape the cruel Mongols, many Koreans fled to the offshore islands where the invaders could not follow because they lacked boats. The Mongols occupied the peninsula for more than a hundred years. They were finally driven from the country by General Yi Taejo who established his own dynasty in 1329. Korea was once again called Choson, and Hanyang, the present city of Seoul, became the capital. The Yi dynasty governed Choson for almost six centuries, until 1910.

During the first centuries of Yi rule, the country made new advances in literature, medicine, astronomy, geology, history, and agriculture. In 1403, some fifty years before Johann Gutenberg invented his printing press, Koreans were printing with movable type. During the same century, Korean scholars developed the *han'gul* writing system. The Chinese ideographs or symbols that the Koreans had been using were so difficult to learn that only a few scholars had mastered them. The simpler *han'gul* made it possible for ordinary people to learn to write.

An astronomical observatory in North Korea, built during the Silla Dynasty about 1300 years ago. Ancient Koreans studied the stars from this stone tower.

4

KOREA AND HER
NEIGHBORS

In the sixteenth century, invaders from the southeast and the north disrupted the peace and prosperity that Koreans had enjoyed for so many years. Japanese soldiers crossed the Korea Strait in thousands of small boats and landed at Pusan in 1592. During the Japanese occupation, which lasted seven years, the Koreans made many unsuccessful attempts to drive the invaders from their homeland. On one occasion, Korean Admiral Yi Sumsen won a famous naval victory over the Japanese by using an ironclad ship shaped like a tortoise.

In 1627, Korean was invaded again, this time by soldiers from Manchuria. Before they withdrew, the invaders forced the Koreans to agree to a limited amount of control by Manchuria. In practice, however, Korea continued to operate as an independent nation.

After their unhappy experiences during the Japanese and Manchurian invasions, the Koreans decided that they wanted no more foreigners in their country. Their resulting isolation from the rest of the world lasted until the 1880's, and Korea came to be known as the Hermit Kingdom.

There were a few foreign visitors during this period, however. In 1653, several Dutch sailors were rescued from a shipwreck off the Korean coast. They may have been the first westerners to visit Korea. Over the years, merchant ships from foreign nations stopped at

The Japanese attack at Song-Hwan, Korea, in 1894.

Korean ports, but the Koreans refused to do any trading. In a few cases, the detested foreigners were killed.

In spite of their refusal to trade with other countries, it became increasingly hard for the Koreans to remain isolated. In 1876, Japan persuaded the Korean government to agree to a treaty of friendship and commerce. In 1882, the United States became the first western nation to conclude a treaty with Korea. Treaties with other countries followed.

Not all Koreans were pleased with their government's decision to admit foreigners and foreign ideas into the country. In 1894, a group called the Tonghaks staged a protest. Lacking a sufficiently strong army of its own, the Korean government asked China to help put down the Tonghaks. China agreed to help and so did Japan, without being asked. The result was a clash between China and Japan.

The Sino-Japanese War was a short one. China was defeated and agreed to recognize Korea's independence. Japan also agreed to recognize Korea's independence, but Japanese soldiers remained in Korea.

Although she was not involved in the Sino-Japanese War, Russia had become an important influence in Korea. To insure her own control of the Korean government, Japan declared war on Russia in 1904. The war, mostly fought outside Korea, ended the following year. The peace treaty, signed at Portsmouth, New Hampshire, made Korea a Japanese protectorate. Japan received the right to help manage Korean affairs and, in return, promised to protect the weaker country. Japanese control of Korea became complete in 1910 when the last Yi emperor, a feeble-minded boy, signed a treaty that annexed his country to Japan.

Most Koreans did not want to be ruled by Japan. In 1919, thirty-

Dr. Syngman Rhee, first president
of the Republic of Korea.

three Korean leaders issued what they called a "Proclamation of Independence," and groups of their countrymen organized peaceful demonstrations against the Japanese. The demonstrations angered Japanese officials who tried to stop them by arresting thousands of Koreans. Some of those arrested were tortured; others were killed. In rural areas, entire villages were burned.

The actions of the Japanese failed to discourage the Koreans, who organized a government of their own with headquarters in Shanghai, China. Dr. Syngman Rhee was elected president of the exiled Korean Provisional Republic, a post he was to hold for many years.

As a young man, Rhee had worked for reforms in the Korean government, an activity that resulted in a sentence of seven years in prison. Upon his release in 1904, Rhee went to the United States where he earned postgraduate degrees from Harvard and Princeton Universities. He was the first Korean to earn a doctorate degree in an American university.

While he was a student, Rhee tried to persuade the United States to help Korea overthrow the Japanese. Although he was unsuccessful, he continued to be a leading spokesman for Korean independence. Because he feared arrest by the Japanese, Rhee remained away from Korea until the end of World War II.

5

A DIVIDED COUNTRY

When World War II ended on August 14, 1945, Russian and American soldiers moved into Korea to supervise the surrender of Japanese troops stationed in that country. The Russians occupied the part of the peninsula north of the 38th parallel of latitude; the United States forces were located south of that line.

The joint occupation, which was intended to be a temporary one, did not go according to plan. When the time came to set up the "free and independent" government that Korea had been promised, the Soviet Union refused to relinquish control of the north. The United States then referred the problem to the newly organized United Nations.

Although their country was a member of the United Nations, Soviet officials refused to let a United Nations commission enter North Korea to supervise elections for a Korean national assembly. Instead of a freely elected government for all of Korea, the Russians wanted the north to have a communist government similar to the government of the Soviet Union.

Elections supervised by the United Nations were held only in South Korea, where the Republic of Korea came into being in 1948. Syngman Rhee, back in Korea after his long exile, was elected president. The United Nations announced that his government was the lawful government of Korea.

Meanwhile, the communist Democratic People's Republic of Korea had been established in the north. Kim Il-sung, a Korean communist, became the premier of the People's Republic.

Kim Il-sung, whose real name is Kim Song Chu, was born in North Korea in 1912. After his father, a schoolmaster, moved his family to Manchuria to escape from Japanese rule, Kim spent several years in Manchuria and China. He joined the Chinese Communist Party and fought as a guerrilla against the Japanese along the Yalu River. Early in World War II, Kim went to the Soviet Union where he received military and political training. Then he joined the Soviet Army and returned to Korea as a Soviet officer in 1945. It was at this time that he adopted the name Kim Il-sung. The original Kim Il-sung was a respected guerrilla leader in the struggle against the Japanese.

Shortly after Kim Il-sung became premier of the Democratic People's Republic of Korea, the Soviet Union announced that it had withdrawn its occupation forces from North Korea. The United States withdrew its forces from South Korea in 1949.

In the year following the withdrawal of United States troops, raiders from North Korea crossed the 38th parallel into South Korea on several occasions. Although their security forces were small, the South Koreans managed to repel the raiders. In June, 1950, however, a strong North Korean force moved into the south. This time the South Koreans could not drive them back.

At the request of the United Nations, sixteen countries agreed to send military help to South Korea. Under the command of the American General Douglas MacArthur, the United Nations forces pushed the Communists back to the 38th parallel. Then the United Nations soldiers fought on until they reached the Chinese border.

China had become a communist nation after World War II. Its government responded to the approach of the United Nations forces by sending large numbers of soldiers to help the North Koreans. To-

(18)

The Armistice Commission is
shown here in session in 1951,
at P'anmunjom, North Korea.
Kim Il-sung, head of the
North Korean Communist government,
is shown seated third from right.

gether, the Chinese and the North Koreans drove the United Nations troops back to the 38th parallel.

Negotiations to end the war in Korea began in July, 1951, but they proceeded slowly because there were so many problems to be solved. When an armistice agreement, signed on July 27, 1953, finally stopped the fighting, the two sides faced each other along a line just north of the 38th parallel. A 2^1/$_2$-mile-wide demilitarized zone was established along this line. The Democratic People's Republic of Korea controlled the area north of the line; the Republic of Korea remained in control in the south.

At the time of the signing of the armistice, it was hoped that a peace conference would soon reunite the two Koreas. However, further discussions failed to produce an agreement and Korea remained a divided country.

To discourge another attack by North Korea, the United States negotiated a mutual security treaty with South Korea. If either country was attacked, the other promised to come to its aid. In addition, the United States promised to give economic assistance to South Korea. The Soviet Union and Communist China offered similar assistance to North Korea.

6

SOUTH KOREA'S
POSTWAR GOVERNMENT

Syngman Rhee, South Korea's first president, was reelected in 1952 and in 1956. His goal remained the freedom and unification of Korea, but his government became despotic and ruthless. Rhee sent the police to arrest his critics and he outlawed the strongest of the political parties that opposed him.

Dr. Rhee was elected again in 1960. However, this time there were widespread complaints that the voting had not been fair. Thousands of students demonstrated against the government's handling of the election. Many of the soldiers who were sent to break up the demonstrations supported the students instead.

Faced with growing opposition and declining support, Dr. Rhee resigned. He left Korea for exile in Hawaii, where he died in 1965 at the age of ninety.

A new South Korean government had been in office only a few months when it was overthrown by a group of army officers led by General Park Chung-hee. Park then became acting president of the military government that ruled the country for two and one-half years. During that time, South Korea's constitution was amended to prepare for a return to civilian rule. The amended constitution increased the power of the president. It also provided for a unicameral, or one-house, national assembly and a court system. Park Chung-hee,

who had retired from the army, was elected president of the Republic of Korea in 1963.

Park, the son of a poor peasant family, grew up in South Korea when the Japanese controlled the country. The Japanese sent him to the Manchukuo Military Academy (Manchukuo is what the Japanese called Manchuria) and to the Japanese Imperial Military Academy in Tokyo. He became a lieutenant in the Japanese Army.

After World War II, Park worked as a civilian intelligence officer for the government of South Korea. He joined the army when the Korean War began and eventually rose to the rank of general.

Park Chung-hee was reelected in 1967 and in 1971, after the constitution was changed to allow a president to serve a third term. In 1972, Park surprised the world by proclaiming martial law in his country. In addition to placing Korea under military rule, he dissolved the National Assembly, banned all political activity, and closed the universities. The president explained that he was forced to act to strengthen the government.

President Park proposed changes in the constitution which would allow the president of South Korea to serve for an unlimited number of six-year terms and would give him much more power, including more control over the National Assembly. The voters of South Korea approved the new constitution by an overwhelming majority. In December, 1972, Park was reelected to the presidency.

Above, South Korea's president Park Chung-hee. A retired Army general, he was elected the Republic's first chief executive in 1963. Below, the Capitol Building of the Republic of Korea in Seoul.

7

NORTH KOREA'S
POSTWAR GOVERNMENT

Durable Kim Il-sung has been premier of the Democratic People's Republic of Korea since 1948. He is also the secretary-general of the Korean Labor Party, the communist party that controls the government.

North Korea's unicameral legislature is called the Supreme People's Assembly. The assembly is supposed to be an important part of the government, but in practice it does little more than approve decisions made elsewhere. According to North Korea's constitution, assembly members are to be elected every four years, although this has not always been done.

North Korea has a court system with a supreme court, provincial courts, and people's courts. It also has a procuracy, a powerful agency whose primary responsibility is to make sure that all citizens obey the law.

In a North Korean city in the early 1950s, giant-sized posters of Kim Il-sung (left) and Soviet Premier Stalin were paraded by the Communists controlling the government.

8

KOREAN FLAGS

The Republic of Korea's flag displays a divided circle (red at the top and blue at the bottom) centered on a white field. A black bar design appears in each corner of the flag.

The Democratic People's Republic of Korea's flag has a wide center strip bordered at the top and bottom by a thin white stripe and a broader blue stripe. At the left of the flag's center is a white disc containing a five-pointed red star. (See the jacket of this book, which displays the chief elements of both flags in its design.)

9

RELIGION IN KOREA

Several religions have influenced the development of the Korean people. The oldest is shamanism and it is one of the few religions that did not come to Korea from some other country.

Shamanism is a form of spirit worship. The ancient Koreans believed in a large number of spirits. There were spirits of the earth, the air, the waters, and the mountains, spirits of the living and the dead, and spirits that lived in rocks and trees. Many spirits were bad and the Koreans believed that they had the power to cause harm unless they were given offerings or warded off in some way. Other spirits were helpful or merely mischievous. The latter spent their time playing tricks on people.

Individuals who were able to "talk" with the spirits were called shamans. They tried to win the friendship of evil spirits in order to influence the spirits' actions. Both men and women could be shamans, but the women shamans, called *mudangs,* were believed to be more powerful.

One of the important ceremonies conducted by the *mudangs* was used to cure the sick. At the beginning of the ceremony, the *mudang* offered food to the spirit believed to be responsible for the illness. Next, the *mudang* performed a ritual dance and asked the spirit to come to her. It was thought that the sick person would recover if the spirit responded and ate some of the food. Then it could be persuaded to leave.

Most Koreans no longer seriously believe in spirits. A few older or uneducated people, especially those living in remote rural areas, still do, however. They call in a *mudang* when someone in the family is sick and they take precautions against evil spirits.

In some Korean villages, there are carved posts that were erected to protect the villages from evil spirits. Roads are crooked because spirits travel in straight lines only. When a house is built, a special ceremony is held to please the house's spirit. On all important occasions, and when things go wrong, the householder offers food and prayer to this spirit.

Confucianism came to Korea from China during the first century B.C. It is not a religion in the strict sense of worshiping a divine being. Rather, it is a code of morals and conduct based on the teachings of the Chinese scholar Confucius.

Confucius, who lived from 551 to 479 B.C., taught that love and goodness were supreme virtues. He stressed the importance of five relationships: between ruler and subject, father and son, husband and wife, older and younger brother, and between friends. For each pair, there was a proper standard of conduct that emphasized the respect that juniors should show their elders.

Beginning in the fourteenth century, when it was adopted as the state religion, Confucianism came to have an important effect on Korean social and political life. It strengthened family ties, gave Koreans a sense of continuity with their past, and encouraged the development of orderly government.

Only the rich have ever had the leisure time to fully carry out the elaborate rules of conduct prescribed by Confucius. Nevertheless, Confucianism continues to have an influence on Korean life.

Like Confucianism, Buddhism came to Korea from China. By the sixth century, it had spread throughout the peninsula. Buddhism is

An elaborate Confucian ceremony being performed
at a South Korean university in 1960.

based on the teachings of an Indian prince who came to be known as the Buddha, or Enlightened One.

Buddhists believe that each person goes through many cycles of life and death. Through good behavior, he gradually reaches higher forms of life. When he becomes religiously perfect, he dies for the final time and enters a state of enlightenment and detachment from the world called nirvana.

Korean Buddhism is a variety called Mahayana, or the Greater Vehicle. A Mahayana Buddhist worships Lord Buddha as the supreme god and he believes in other Buddhist gods as well. Rather than nirvana, his goal is to enter a special kind of heaven.

Buddhism flourished in Korea until the fourteenth century when Confucianism became the state religion. Buddhism continued to be an important religion, however, and it remains one today. Buddha's teachings about equality among people and reincarnation after death have been especially influential in shaping Korean life.

Korea is dotted with Buddhist temples, monasteries, pagodas, and large stone figures of Buddha. About a thousand temples are still in use.

Christianity made its first appearance in Korea at the end of the sixteenth century when the Japanese invaded the peninsula. The first Christian missionaries, who were Roman Catholic priests from China, came to Korea in 1686.

Soon, the new religion had won enough converts among scholars and common people to alarm government officials. They regarded Christianity, or Western Learning, as a threat to Confucianism. In 1786, Christianity was banned and for many years its believers were

Above, an ancient Buddhist temple at Kongju. Allied military personnel often visit this historic Korean landmark, second largest of its kind, and a popular shrine. Below, a Buddhist priest beats a sacred temple drum during a religious ceremony.

(31)

persecuted. Between 1865 and 1868, eight thousand Catholics, about half of the total number, were executed.

Christian missionaries returned to Korea after the treaty of commerce and friendship with the United States was signed in 1882. Both Protestant and Catholic missionaries won many converts. They opened churches, schools, and hospitals. One important result of their activity was a better understanding of the West by the formerly isolated Koreans.

Some Koreans belong to a religious movement known as Ch'ondogyo, or Teaching of the Heavenly Way. When it was started in 1860 as an alternative to Catholicism, it was called Tonghak, or Eastern Learning. Followers of Ch'ondogyo were called Tonghaks, and it was this group that protested against admitting foreigners to Korea in 1894.

Ch'ondogyo has borrowed ideas from other religions, including Catholicism. It stresses the equality of man and the unity of man and the universe. Ch'ondogyo rituals include putting aside a spoonful of rice each day for the church and setting out clean water as a symbol of the shedding of the blood of Ch'oe Che-u, the great Ch'ondogyo teacher. Ch'oe Che-u was arrested in 1864 and executed as a heretic.

In the Republic of Korea, freedom of religion is guaranteed by the constitution, although the government tries to discourage spirit worship. The constitution of the Democratic People's Republic of Korea recognizes the "freedom of religious beliefs and of conducting religious services," but in practice Kim Il-sung's government regards religion as unscientific and a relic of Korea's past. Only the Ch'ondogyo faith has received limited government approval.

A Catholic church in downtown Seoul,
one of many in the Republic of Korea.

10

CHANGING STYLES
IN DRESS

In Korea's cities and towns, particularly in the south, most people now wear western-style dress. Older people in rural areas still cling to traditional clothing, however, and on holidays and special occasions even city dwellers don their native dress.

Men in traditional dress wear wide trousers tightly bound at the waist with colored bands. Sometimes the trousers are also gathered at the ankles. The jacket is short, loose, and fastened with a band tied in a bow. On formal occasions a man may wear a long, flowing coat called a *turumagi*. Older Korean men wear tall black hats made of horsehair and silk. Originally the hat was designed to cover a topknot; today it is a symbol of age and dignity.

Traditional Korean dress for women consists of a long, pleated skirt, a tight inner jacket, and a short bolero with long sleeves.

Both men and women frequently wear white clothing. In ancient Korea, white was the color worn by the common people. It was also worn during lengthy periods of mourning following the death of

A variety of clothing is to be seen in Korea. Above, sales people in western dress demonstrate their wares. Below, a Korean family in traditional white clothing, are questioned by American and Korean military police.

(34)

royalty. As a result, Koreans became accustomed to wearing white.

Cotton is the material most often used in Korean clothing. For winter wear, the cotton is quilted.

In North Korea, many people wear standardized work uniforms, student uniforms, or uniforms similar to the one worn by Mao Tse-tung, the chairman of the Chinese Communist Party. Clothing is manufactured and distributed by the government. The quality and amount of clothing each person receives is determined by his occupation. In some cases the clothing is free.

11

HOW KOREANS LIVE

Traditional Korean dwellings are simple, one-story structures of brick or stone built in the shape of an "L" or "U." On the outside the upper part of the walls is plastered with a mixture of clay and straw. The gently sloping roof is thatched with rice stalks. However, if a family is well-to-do, the roof may be tiled.

The number and size of the rooms in a Korean house vary with the prosperity of the owner. The basic rooms are the kitchen, bedroom, and living room; others are added as they are needed and as the family can afford them.

Koreans have had radiant heating in their houses for fifteen hundred years. Before the floors are laid, a network of flues or channels is dug beneath the house. The flues are covered with large, flat stones topped with a layer of clay. The family walks on heavy brown paper laid on top of the clay. Each room may have its own fire pot from which hot air and smoke travel through the flues to a chimney, or one fire pot may supply heat to several rooms.

Because of the heating system, the floor is the warmest place in a Korean house. Koreans, therefore, developed the custom of eating at very low tables. They sit on mats or cushions and sleep on bedding laid on the floor.

In Korea, household furnishings are apt to be few and simple. A visitor to a typical kitchen would see little more than a stove and

the jars, pots, bowls, and utensils used in cooking. There are no beds in the bedrooms. The quilts and other bedding, placed on the floor at night, are rolled up during the day. They may be stored on top of a wooden cabinet. The living room generally contains a cabinet, perhaps a low dining table, and a straw mat with a few pillows. Wall hangings provide a decorative note.

The homes of well-to-do Koreans have several rooms. The room to the right of the entrance is where the head of the house eats his meals and entertains his guests. The other members of the family eat in a dining room. In addition to a master bedroom and a guestroom, there are bedrooms for other family members.

Koreans remove their shoes before entering a house. By doing this, they preserve the paper floors which Korean housewives like to keep as smooth and glistening as linoleum. Removing shoes also protects the polished wood floors used in some rooms.

In South Korea's larger cities, especially in higher income districts, builders are now putting up multi-story houses. In several cities, the government has constructed high-rise apartment buildings to help ease the country's housing shortage.

North Korea has also suffered from a housing shortage. Shortly after the end of the Korean conflict, Kim Il-sung's government announced a plan to build enough houses to replace those destroyed during the war and to take care of the needs of a growing population. According to reports from North Korea, much new housing has been built. However, the system used to assign living quarters indicates that more housing is needed.

In North Korea's cities, housing is divided into five classes ranging from units with one room and half-size kitchens to relatively large houses with gardens. General laborers and office workers are as-

A typical thatch-roofed house
in the Korean countryside.

signed to the former, while the latter are reserved for top-ranking government and Communist Party officials. In between these two groups, factory foremen, schoolteachers, school principals, factory managers, college professors, actors, and those in other occupations are assigned to housing according to the importance of the job they hold. Those with the lowest salaries pay the lowest rents, but all rents are low by western standards.

Once a North Korean has been assigned to a house or apartment, he cannot move until he has been promoted to a better job. The size of his family has no effect on his housing assignment.

Korean women "iron" clothes in a typical woman's room of a Korean house.

12

KOREAN FOOD IS
HIGHLY SEASONED

Kimch'i is the Korean national dish. Like many Korean foods, it is highly seasoned. A combination of vegetables and strong spices, *kimch'i* is served with most meals.

Korean cooks make several kinds of *kimch'i*. They use cabbage, long radish-like tubers called *daikon,* or cucumbers, to which they add leeks, onions, spices, hot peppers, salt, and other ingredients, depending on the kind of *kimch'i* desired. In the fall, Koreans prepare pickled *kimch'i*. Layers of *daikon,* soy sauce, leeks, onions, salt, spices, and possibly peppers are placed in a large earthenware jar. After several weeks, the *kimch'i* is ready to eat. Some families make a whole year's supply of pickled *kimch'i* at one time.

Winter *kimch'i* is also made in large quantities in the fall and stored in jars. It contains both cabbage and *daikon*. The cabbage grown in Korea is long in shape, rather than round, with leaves that turn outward at the top. Sometimes it is called Chinese cabbage.

Rice is the principal food in the Korean diet. A Korean thinks he has eaten well if his meal has included rice. When other grains such as barley, wheat, or millet are eaten, they are mixed with rice if

Dried fish is a favorite food of Koreans. Here fish are being hung up to dry at a coastal fishing village.

possible. Poor people who cannot afford rice every day try to have rice on New Year's Day and on their birthdays.

Good Korean cooks prepare rice very carefully. They wash it several times and cook it in an iron pot in just the right amount of water. When the rice is removed from the cooking pot, water is added to the burned rice remaining on the bottom. The resulting mixture, called *sungyong* or rice tea, is served after the meal.

During the summer, Koreans eat a variety of fresh fruits and vegetables. Persimmons, peaches, pears, melons, apples, and berries are plentiful. Among the vegetables, potatoes, cabbage, *daikon,* turnips, hot peppers, leeks, and beans are especially popular. Both fruits and vegtables are pickled for winter use.

Fish is eaten throughout Korea. It may be fresh, salted, or dried. Fresh fish is sometimes served raw. Meat is expensive and not widely eaten. Eggs are considered a delicacy.

Koreans eat from small bowls, generally made of brass. Rice is usually eaten with a spoon, but chopsticks are used for *kimch'i* and other foods which have been cut into pieces. Soup, a winter favorite, may be drunk from a bowl or eaten with a spoon. Koreans consider it bad manners to scratch a bowl with a spoon or chopsticks or to click either instrument against the teeth.

13

SOME KOREAN HOLIDAYS

Korea officially follows the Gregorian calendar, the calendar that is used in the United States and in Europe. However, many Korean holidays originated centuries ago when a calendar based on the phases of the moon was used. The lunar calendar is more variable than the Gregorian calendar. Thus, the date of Lunar New Year's Day, the beginning of one of Korea's principal holidays, falls in late January or early February, depending on the year.

Traditionally, Koreans celebrate Lunar New Year's Day with a feast to their ancestors. During the next two weeks, they visit friends, eat holiday foods, listen to favorite music, and participate in kite-flying, tug-of-war, and wrestling contests. Koreans also celebrate the New Year's Day that falls on January 1.

On March 1, the anniversary of the day in 1919 when thirty-three Korean patriots presented a "Declaration of Independence" to the Japanese who controlled their country, Koreans observe *Samil* or Independence Day.

May Day, on May 1, observed in many countries as Labor Day, is one of North Korea's four national holidays. Liberation Day, on August 15, is another national holiday in North Korea. It commemorates the end of World War II when Korea was liberated from Japanese rule. August 15 is the occasion for a double celebration in

South Korea because it is also the date on which the Republic of Korea was founded in 1948.

North Korea celebrates its Founding Day on September 9 with a national holiday. (New Year's Day on January 1 is the fourth national holiday in North Korea.) Other days observed in North Korea include the Day of the People's Army, on February 8; April 25, commemorating the day that Kim Il-sung and other Korean Communists organized anti-Japanese guerrilla units in 1932; July 27, celebrating "victory" in 1953 in the "Patriotic War against the United States"; and October 10, the Founding Day of the Korean Worker's Party in 1945.

The Republic of Korea's first constitution was promulgated on July 17, 1948, and that date is celebrated each year in South Korea as Constitution-Making Day. Armed Forces Day, on October 1, is observed much as it is in the United States. National Foundation Day on October 3 honors the legendary Tan'gun who founded Korea as a nation. On October 9, *Han'gul*, or Alphabet, Day marks the anniversary of the introduction of the *han'gul* writing system in 1446. The day is also observed in North Korea. October 24 is United Nations Day when South Korean and United Nations officials take part in ceremonies at Seoul's Capital Plaza and at the United Nations Cemetery near Pusan where many of the dead of the Korean War are buried.

Korea's lunar holidays are festive occasions. Buddha's Birthday, which falls on the eighth day of the fourth lunar month (late May), is traditionally celebrated with elaborate rituals at temples and the display of many lanterns. Another traditional observance, the *Tano*

Harvest Moon Festival, in late September, is the Korean counterpart of America's Thanksgiving Day. Here, near Seoul, entire families have recently taken to visiting and picnicking at family grave sites.

Festival, marks the end of plowing. *Tano,* on the fifth day of the fifth lunar month (mid-June), is noted for its swinging contests in which women and girls compete for prizes.

Korea's *Ch'usok,* or Harvest Moon Festival, on the fifteenth day of the eighth lunar month (late September), comes at the end of the harvest season. It is celebrated with family reunions and visits to family tombs. During the day, there are contests and games; at night, people go out to view the full moon. The traditional *Ch'usok* dish is *song-pym,* a half-moon-shaped rice cake filled with sweet and salted bean paste and steamed with pine needles.

Christians in the Republic of Korea, who number well over 1.5 million, celebrate Christmas as it is celebrated in the West. In the Democratic People's Republic of Korea, where the government dis-courages all religious celebrations, Christmas is not observed. The number of Christians in North Korea was greatly reduced after World War II when many of them fled to the south to escape com-munist rule.

14

GAMES ARE POPULAR

Koreans of all ages have always been fond of games. They enjoy soccer, wrestling, table tennis, judo, swimming, ice skating, skiing, sledding, weight lifting, bowling, and a game that resembles field hockey. Card games and games similar to chess and checkers are also popular.

Children play tag, hide-and-seek, and blindman's bluff. Little girls play house and make paper dolls. Boys play games with balls and sticks.

Traditionally, the Korean skies have been filled with kites during the first two weeks of the Lunar New Year. Then the kites are cut loose and allowed to fly away. The kite flyers hope that this will ward off evil during the year.

The beginning of the new year is also the traditional time for pairs of girls and women to engage in a contest in which they jump up and down on the ends of a seesaw. The object is to jump gracefully without falling off.

Swinging is another sport favored by Korean girls. The swings are higher than American swings and the swinging is done standing up. Villages and towns hold swinging festivals during *Tano* and thousands of spectators turn out to watch the fun.

(49)

Many Koreans are too busy making a living to devote much time to recreation. Moreover, they lack the money to buy equipment. Their few leisure hours are apt to be spent visiting friends and relatives, telling stories, singing, and playing simple games.

One of the most popular sporting contests in Korea is swinging.
Here a swinging contest is attended by thousands
on the Due Su Palace grounds in Seoul.

15

KOREAN TIME

Because Korea is west of the international date line, it is always a day ahead of the United States. When it is Monday noon in Seoul, the capital of the Republic of Korea, it is 10:30 P.M. on Sunday in Washington, D.C.; 9:30 P.M. in Chicago, Illinois; 8:30 P.M. in Denver, Colorado; and 7:30 P.M. in San Francisco, California.

16

MANY KOREANS
ARE FARMERS

Approximately half of Korea's workers are engaged in farming and related activities. They are concentrated in the peninsula's river valleys and coastal plains where the best agricultural land is located. Only about 20 percent of the peninsula's area is suitable for farming; the remainder is too mountainous.

Rice is Korea's most important crop. It grows in a small field called a paddy, a name that is also given to the rice plant. Low banks of earth or dikes enclose the paddies which are located where they can be flooded with two to four inches of freshwater.

Work on South Korea's rice crop begins in the early spring when the farmers spread fertilizer over the paddies and plow them. Sleek-haired oxen pull the plows through soil which is covered with about two inches of water. Each farmer selects his most fertile paddies and prepares them for the rice seeds which he will plant by hand with the help of his wife. While the seedlings are growing, the beds are weeded every five days or so.

At transplanting time, the farmer and his wife remove the shoots, one at a time, by grasping each blade close to the mud. They are collected in the opposite hand until it is full. Then the shoots are tied with a piece of rice straw for removal to the growing fields.

Transplanting the rice is also done by hand and it takes many

days, even though neighbors form groups to help one another. The seedlings are placed, three or more at a time, in a hole that the planter makes with his finger. Children help in this work by holding a line to guide the men planting the rice. The farmer whose paddies are being planted provides food for the workers.

Water covers the paddies during transplanting and they remain submerged for most of the growing season. When he cultivates his rice, using a short-handled tool shaped something like a sickle, the farmer works in mud. He disturbs frogs and snakes as he moves between the rows of rice. Sometimes bloodsuckers attach themselves to the farmer's feet and legs.

As the rice grows, the paddies change in color from light green to dark green. At harvest time, they are a golden yellow.

Rice is harvested by hand with a sharp sickle. The harvesters leave the cut rice on the ground which is now drained of water. When the rice has dried, it is formed into sheaves and stacked along the dikes for further drying. Then it is carried home and threshing begins.

Neighbors help one another at threshing time because many hands are needed. Farmers who use the old method of threshing tie a piece of rope around a sheaf of rice and beat the sheaf against a block of wood or some other object to knock loose the grains of rice. Other farmers may use a foot-powered revolving drum covered with teeth to remove the rice grains.

The threshed rice must be winnowed to free it of chaff, or husks. This is done by slowly sliding the rice off the edge of a winnowing tray to let the wind blow the chaff away. If there is no wind, the workers must create some by fanning the falling rice with a mat or a foot-powered fan. Finally the threshed rice is put into straw bags to be stored until it is sold or needed for the kitchen.

No part of the rice plant is wasted. The straw that remains after

Korean farmers at work in a rice field.

Here, Korean farmers husk their harvested rice —
their staple diet — on local threshing machines.

the rice is threshed is made into bags and rope. It is used for the thatched roofs that cover many Korean houses and in the manufacture of hats, sandals, raincoats, brooms, brushes, and baskets. Even the hulls, removed when the rice grains are prepared for cooking, are used — for fuel, fertilizer, and packing material and in the manufacture of rayon.

In the southern part of Korea, mild winters allow a farmer to plant a second crop in his paddy fields. Often he plants barley or wheat. This time, however, he does not flood the paddies. He harvests the extra crop before it is time to transplant rice shoots in the spring.

Other important crops grown by the farmers of South Korea are millet, corn, vegetables, tobacco, hemp, fruit, and cotton. Some farmers raise mulberry trees to supply food for silkworms.

South Korean farms are small, averaging just over two acres in size. Most farms are divided into tiny plots in each of which a different crop is grown. Because much of what a farmer produces is consumed at home, his cash income is low. For that reason, more and more Korean children are moving to the city in search of better-paying jobs.

In North Korea, individual farmers do not own or rent land. Instead, farm land is the property of the state. It is organized into some 3,800 cooperatives that may be as large as a thousand acres each with about three hundred families living on them. Farm workers belong to brigades, or teams, and each team receives daily orders about the work to be done. The farmers are paid in cash and in crops. What each man receives depends on the amount of labor he contributed. But before the workers can be paid, the cooperative must deliver a certain portion of its produce to the government.

As in South Korea, rice is the major crop. Wheat, corn, grain sorghums, cotton, tobacco, potatoes, and other vegetables are grown in areas not suited to rice cultivation.

17

INDUSTRY CAME LATE
TO KOREA

Korea was a land of farmers when Japan occupied the peninsula in 1910. At first, the Japanese exploited their new possession as a source of rice and raw materials for the Japanese homeland and Korea remained an almost exclusively agricultural country. After 1931, however, the Japanese encouraged the development of manufacturing, but they allowed the Koreans to produce only those products that Japan needed. Because most of Korea's minerals, coal, and sources of hydroelectric power were located in the north, heavy industries, such as mining and the production of steel, cement, and fertilizer, were concentrated in that region. Textile mills and other light industries were located in the south.

The Korean conflict destroyed many of the country's industries. After the armistice, the division of the peninsula at the 38th parallel made recovery difficult in both the Republic of Korea and in the Democratic People's Republic of Korea. South Korea was left with 75 percent of the good farming land, but only light industries. North Korea had two-thirds of all Korean industry, 90 percent of the peninsula's hydroelectric power, and much of its coal, iron, minerals, and forests.

Population was unevenly divided as well. Approximately 17,000,-000 people, or roughly two-thirds of the total population, remained

The Hankuk Fertilizer Plant at Ulsan, Korea, went into operation in 1967.
It is the largest one of its kind in the Orient.

North Korean workers put rubber shoes into an oven to harden after they have been put together by Korean women workers. Shoes are among North Korea's leading manufactured products.

in the south. A 1953 census counted 8,491,000 people in North Korea. By 1970, South Korea's population had climbed to 31,469,132. The estimated 1970 population of North Korea was 14,000,000.

The United States assisted South Korea in a successful effort to rebuild and expand its economy. Today, products formerly obtained from the north are manufactured in the south and government-owned power plants have been constructed throughout the country to supply vital electric energy. Food processing and the manufacturing of textiles, clothing, chemicals, ceramics, metal products, and transport equipment rank among the largest industries. Clothing, plywood, and textiles are the leading exports. The United States is South Korea's best customer, followed by Japan.

Of the fifty different kinds of minerals produced in South Korea, anthracite coal, iron ore, tungsten, gold, graphite, fluorite, and salt are the most important. The country has no known oil resources and all of its oil must be imported.

When the Communists came into power in North Korea after World War II, they launched a program designed to expand the country's industries as rapidly as possible. The Korean conflict interrupted that program, however, and left much of the north in ruins. In 1953, Premier Kim Il-sung's government made a new start toward industrial development. Help in the form of loans, grants, technicians, and equipment came from the Soviet Union, the People's Republic of China, and other communist countries. Since then, North Korea's industrial growth has been steady. The manufacture of machinery, metal processing, and mining have received the highest priority, but light industry and the production of consumer goods have increased also, especially in recent years.

In North Korea, all industries are operated by the government and all workers are government employees. Workers are assigned to jobs where they are needed most and for which they are best suited. For example, young and strong workers are given jobs in mining, fishing, and lumbering. Women, who make up about half of the labor force, work primarily in light industry and in educational fields.

North Korea suffers from a shortage of trained labor. There have never been enough workers to carry out Premier Kim Il-sung's ambitious plans for the development of the country. Nevertheless, progress has been substantial.

Among North Korea's leading manufactured products are machinery, metal products, textiles, shoes, food products, and chemicals. North Korea has large deposits of coal, iron ore, lead, zinc, copper, gold, graphite, silver, and tungsten. The government has given high priority to the production of coal and iron ore, both of which are important to the development of heavy industry. The hydroelectric power system has also received special attention. Besides furnishing power and lighting, North Korea's extensive hydroelectric system, with its reservoirs and dams, plays an important role in water conservation, irrigation, and flood control.

The Soviet Union and the People's Republic of China are North Korea's most important trading partners. Processed metal and chemical products, mineral ores, and machinery head the list of North Korean exports. Oil, machinery, and chemical and rubber goods are her chief imports.

18

SOUTH KOREA'S
CITIES

SEOUL | Seoul, the capital of the Republic of Korea, is located in the northwestern part of the country, about thirty miles inland from the Yellow Sea. Four mountains ring the city: the Namsan on the south, the Naksan on the east, the Inwagsan on the west, and the Pukhansan on the north. The Han River flows westward through Seoul.

In Seoul, winters are cold; there are three months with average temperatures below freezing. Summers, on the other hand, are warm, with temperatures averaging above sixty-eight degrees Fahrenheit during the four warmest months. Seoul receives most of its rainfall in late summer. Winters are dry.

Because of its nearness to the 38th parallel separating North and South Korea, Seoul came under heavy attack during the Korean War. On two occasions it was occupied by Communist forces. When the fighting ceased, more than 80 percent of the city had suffered war damage. Korea's Capitol Building, which resembles the United States Capitol in Washington, was almost totally destroyed. It has been rebuilt and now houses government offices. South Korea's legislature meets in the National Assembly Building in central Seoul.

South Korea's president lives and works in *Chong Wa Dae,* or Blue

House, also located in central Seoul. *Chong Wa Dae* receives its name from the unusual blue color of its tiled roof.

Extensive rebuilding after the Korean War has turned Seoul into a modern city with broad streets, freeways, a subway line, shopping arcades, and tall buildings housing offices and banks.

Some of Seoul's six million residents live in new apartments; others live in charming L-shaped houses grouped in clusters resembling small villages. But the city's poor inhabitants are crowded into shacks in Seoul's slums. The very poor have no houses at all. At night they sleep in the streets, in the pedestrian tunnels beneath busy intersections, or in the city's open sewers when the weather is dry.

Many poor families came to Seoul from the country hoping to make a better living in the city. Not all of them found steady employment. Most of South Korea's cities experienced rapid growth during the 1950's and 1960's as farmers moved to urban areas. The refugees who left North Korea after World War II also settled in the cities, largely in Seoul.

Yi T'ae-jo, the first ruler of Korea's Yi dynasty, chose Seoul (then called Hanyang) as his capital in 1392. For protection, he surrounded the city with a stone wall twenty to thirty feet high. Eight gates pierced the wall. Portions of the wall and three gates still stand. One of the gates, *Nam-dae-moon,* the Great South Gate, is located in the center of the street leading from Seoul Railway Station and thus continues to serve as an entrance to the city. However, traffic now flows around the gate rather than through it. *Nam-dae-moon,* with its massive granite walls and curving tiled roof, is considered an architectural masterpiece.

South Korea's capital of Seoul,
showing the famous Great South Gate,
oldest structure in the city.

Seoul contains many reminders of Korea's colorful past. Kymbok (Pleasant Happiness) Palace, in the northern part of the city, was begun by Yi T'ae-jo in 1394. Some five hundred buildings were once located within the palace walls. The Japanese destroyed Kymbok Palace when they invaded Korea in 1592, but the Koreans rebuilt it during the 1860's. No longer as large as it was in the days of the early Yi rulers, Kymbok Palace now has a throne room, a ten-story pagoda, and several lovely ponds and pavilions.

Changdok (Prosperous Virtue) Palace is considered the most beautiful of Seoul's ancient palaces. Its fifty-six buildings and its grounds are now a national shrine. Built in 1404, Changdok Palace became the royal residence after the destruction of Kymbok Palace. Changdok Palace is famous for its Secret Garden whose beautiful lotus pools, pleasure pavilions, and winding paths were constructed to amuse the Yi rulers of Korea. Today, ordinary Koreans enjoy the Secret Garden.

Duk-Soo (Virtuous Longevity) Palace, in the center of Seoul, served as the residence of the Yi kings during the last 280 years of the dynasty. It is the smallest of the surviving Yi palaces. Today the National Museum occupies one of the buildings on the beautifully landscaped palace grounds. The museum displays thousands of paintings and works of sculpture and ceramics, some of them 2,000 years old.

Tiny Pagoda Park, located near Duk-Soo Palace, received its name from a beautiful thirteen-story pagoda built there in 1497. The pagoda is still standing. The park is also famous as the place where the thirty-three Korean patriots read their declaration of independence in 1919 to protest Japanese control of their country. The citizens of Seoul like to walk and rest in Pagoda Park. The park also attracts musicians, herb sellers, fortune-tellers, and speakers.

Nearby is Jongmyo, the Imperial Ancestral Temple, where the ancestral tablets of the Yi dynasty are preserved. The temple was erected in 1395.

Modern Seoul centers on Chongno Street with its concentration of department stores, banks, restaurants, and tailors' shops. Another main thoroughfare, Taipyong Street, running between the Great South Gate and the Capitol Building, is lined with government buildings, foreign legations, and newspaper offices.

Most of Seoul's industries are located in Yongtung-po on the city's west side. Here factory workers produce electrical fixtures, farm implements, textiles, rubber shoes, and other consumer goods.

Approximately half of South Korea's college-level schools are in Seoul. They are primarily private schools, but in South Korea private schools receive some assistance from the government. One of Seoul's universities, Songgyonggwan, is a noted center of Confucian scholarship. The university was founded in 1397. On its campus is a stone tablet erected by a Yi king in 1742. The inscription on the stone reads: "The man of virtue fighteth not, the man of small mind understandeth not."

Seoul is the hub of South Korea's transportation system. Railroads and highways radiate in all directions from the city. Seoul's busy Kimpo International Airport is served by several foreign airlines and by the government-operated Korea Air Line. The latter provides frequent service between the capital and South Korea's principal cities.

INCHON | Inchon, twenty-four miles west of Seoul, is the capital's seaport and one of South Korea's major ports. Although some farms and apple orchards remain, the countryside between Seoul and Inchon is fast becoming industrialized.

Ships from many countries call at Inchon to pick up the industrial and agricultural products of the Seoul area. Road and rail traffic between Seoul and Inchon is heavy as trucks and trains deliver goods to the harbor and return with products imported into the country.

Inchon's thirty-foot tidal range, the distance between high tide and low tide, is one of the largest in the world. The ebb and flow of the tides is fascinating to watch, but at low tide ships cannot use some of Inchon's docks.

More than 500,000 Koreans live in Inchon. Some of them work in the city's iron, steel, and chemical industries. Others work on the docks or make their living as fishermen. Fishing is good in the waters near Inchon. South Korea also has a deep-sea fishing fleet that travels as far away as the Atlantic Ocean to catch tuna for export to other countries.

On September 15, 1950, Inchon was the site of the famous amphibious landing that allowed United Nations forces under General Douglas MacArthur to retake Seoul from the Communists and advance into North Korea. A statue of General MacArthur stands in the grounds of Inchon's Mangook Park.

The residents of Inchon are fortunate in having numerous islands, noted for their beauty and excellent sand beaches, within easy reach of their city.

PUSAN | South Korea's chief port is Pusan, on the southeastern coast. Pusan has one of the finest and largest natural harbors in the Far East and its bustling docks handle more than five million tons of cargo annually.

Pusan's importance as a port dates from the Japanese occupation of Korea. The Japanese developed Pusan, which they called Fusan, as their main gateway to the peninsula. A regular ferry service oper-

*A city street in Pusan,
South Korea's chief port.*

ated between Shimonosiki in Japan and Pusan. From Pusan, rail lines ran northward to Manchuria and China.

During the Korean War, Pusan was the temporary capital of the Republic of Korea. Because the city escaped major war damage, it was flooded with refugees who lived in wooden shacks on the city's hills. After several disastrous fires in the refugee camps, the areas were rebuilt with more substantial dwellings.

Pusan's two million inhabitants make it South Korea's second largest city. They work in a variety of industries including ship-building, iron and steel, railroad shops, textile manufacturing, rice milling, and salt refining. Most of Pusan's mills and factories and its commercial establishments are located in the eastern part of the city.

Pusan National University and Tong-A (Eastern Asia) University are located in Pusan. They rank among South Korea's major univer-sities. On the city's outskirts are two of the oldest and most impres-sive Buddhist temples in Korea. They are Pumee, the Temple of the Sacred Fish, and Tongdo-Sa, the Temple of the Universal Salvation.

Seven miles north of Pusan is one of South Korea's popular resort areas, Tongnai, which is famous for its hot springs. People come from all over the country to enjoy the curative effects of the springs and Tongnai's beautiful scenery and many cabarets.

Pusan is a departure point for Cheju Island, some fifty miles off the southwestern tip of the Korean peninsula. The semi-tropical is-land is dominated by Mount Halla, an extinct volcano. Hunters seek-ing pheasants visit Cheju in the autumn. The island's most popular attraction, however, is its women divers who, even in the winter, dive for abalone, conch, sea cucumber, and kelp. Wearing goggles and suits made of white cloth, the divers work from ten to twenty yards offshore. They can descend as deep as fifty feet and remain submerged for three or four minutes.

KYONGJU | Kyongju (Pleasant City), some fifty miles north of Pusan, was the capital of the ancient Silla kingdom. At one time, the city may have had as many as a million inhabitants; its present population is 300,000.

Many relics of its former glory remain in Kyongju. Museums display gold crowns that belonged to long-dead Silla kings, beautiful works of art, and a great bronze bell that once hung in the tower of a Buddhist temple. The bell, cast in the year 771, weighs about seventy-nine tons. It is one of the largest bells of its kind in the world.

Tombs and temples abound in the Kyongju area. The burial grounds of the Silla kings are located near the city. Pulguk Temple, erected in A.D. 540, was once one of the largest Buddhist centers in Asia. Sokkuram Cave contains a temple with an unusual white stone image of Buddha. It is one of the great masterpieces of Silla art. Boolkooska, a temple dating from the eighth century, has a gold image of Buddha that is twenty-five feet tall.

Kyongju's ancient stone observatory, Chomsongdae, built in 647, is one of the oldest observatories in the world. It is still in excellent condition.

TAEGU | Taegu, with a population of 850,000, is South Korea's third largest city. Located about forty miles west of Kyongju, Taegu is the regional center of an area that has the highest population density in the Republic of Korea. The country's average population density is a crowded 1247.8 persons per square mile. This is greater than the population density of Japan, which is 1083.4 persons per square mile. The figure for the United States is 84.9 persons. North Korea's population density is 301 persons per square mile.

The major railway line connecting Seoul and Pusan passes through

A street market in the business section of Taegu,
South Korea's third-largest city.

Taegu, and the city has become the collection and distribution center for a rich agricultural region. Because winters are mild here, two crops can be grown each year. Mines near Taegu produce copper and tungsten and the city is a textile manufacturing center.

One of Korea's most important Buddhist treasures is preserved at Haein-Sa, a temple twenty-eight miles west of Taegu. It consists of 81,240 wooden printing tablets that were used by Buddhist monks during the thirteenth century to produce a scripture. The tablets took sixteen years to complete.

19

NORTH KOREA'S CITIES

PYONGYANG | Pyongyang, the capital of the Democratic People's Republic of Korea, lies about thirty miles up the Taedong River from the Yellow Sea. Unlike most of North Korea, which is mountainous, the region around Pyongyang is relatively flat. Because of its exposed location, Pyongyang receives the full force of winter winds blowing from the cold Asian landmass. The city's average January temperature is 17.6 degrees Fahrenheit. Summer temperatures average in the seventies. June, July, and August are the months of heaviest rainfall.

Koreans proudly state that there may have been a city at Pyongyang's location as early as 1122 B.C. when Kija, the Chinese sage, came to Korea. Kija is believed to have established his capital at Pyongyang. His grave is said to be somewhere north of the city, although no trace of it has ever been found.

But Chinese graves from a later period have been discovered near Pyongyang. The artifacts found in those graves tell us that highly civilized people were living in the Pyongyang area as early as the second century B.C. They worked with metal and bronze, and they were familiar with Chinese writing and Confucian scriptures.

Pyongyang was a thriving capital city until the seventh century when Kyongju, the capital of the Silla kings, replaced it as a government center. Pyongyang remained the political and educational cen-

A view of Pyongyang, capital of the
Democratic People's Republic of Korea
and an important industrial center.

ter of northwestern Korea, however. After the formation of the Democratic People's Republic of Korea in 1948, Pyongyang once again became a capital city.

During the Korean War, Pyongyang was almost totally destroyed. The rebuilt city has block after block of apartment houses, handsome boulevards, and many parks. A 600-foot radio and television tower with a large viewing platform dominates the skyline. Almost as prominent is the sixty-foot-tall bronze statue of Premier Kim Il-sung that stands in a plaza in front of the Museum of the Korean Revolution. The statue is visible for miles when it is floodlighted at night.

Pyongyang's Moranbong sports stadium seats 70,000 people. Another important civic building, the Grand Theater, features performances by Korean singers and dancers. Both structures were completed in 1960.

Some of Pyongyang's most famous temples have been rebuilt in their original form. They are popular tourist attractions, as are the surviving royal pavilions and the remains of the old city walls and gates.

More than one million Koreans live in Pyongyang. They work in iron and steel mills, textile plants, and factories that produce chemicals, automotive vehicles of various kinds, electrical equipment, and many other items. Fifteen thousand students are enrolled in Pyongyang's Kim Il-sung University.

Pyongyang is the center of North Korea's railroad system, which provides the country's principal means of transportation. Because gasoline for cars and trucks must be imported, an extensive system of highways has not been developed in the north. Many of the existing roads are unpaved. Shipping along its coasts and on its rivers supplements North Korea's busy railroads. Pyongyang has port facilities on the Taedong River to handle waterborne freight.

Sunan Airport, about ten miles north of Pyongyang, is North

Korea's international airport. From Sunan there are usually sched-
uled flights to Peking and Moscow. North Korea's civil airline, which
is controlled by the air force, also flies between Pyongyang and the
country's major cities.

KAESONG | Kaesong, with more than 139,000 residents, is another
of Korea's former capitals that has survived to become a bustling,
modern city. It became Korea's capital during the tenth century and
for two hundred years thrived as a political and cultural center.
Royal tombs and ancient city walls remain from that period.

Located just south of the 38th parallel and about fifteen miles in-
land from the Yellow Sea, Kaesong was in the thick of the fighting
during the Korean War. It changed hands several times, but when
the armistice ended the hostilities, it was held by the Communists.

Today Kaesong is a trade center for the medicinal herb ginseng,
and for the barley, rice, and wheat grown on nearby collective farms.

HAMHUNG and HUNGNAM | Hamhung and the neighboring Sea of
Japan port of Hungnam, with a combined population of more than
420,000, make up North Korea's second largest urban area.

The availability of hydroelectric power led to the industrial development of Hamhung and Hungnam. The former was an old commercial and government center, but Hungnam began as a small fishing
village. Hamhung and Hungnam have become a center for North
Korea's chemical industry which requires large amounts of power.

CH'ONGJIN | Ch'ongjin, on North Korea's northeastern coast, is the
country's third largest city. More than 265,000 Koreans live in
Ch'ongjin, which is both a major port and an important steel pro-
ducer.

Iron ore is readily available to Ch'ongjin by way of a railroad that

(77)

connects the city with iron mines along the Tumen River. The mines and Ch'ongjin's steel industry were originally developed by the Japanese and they have been expanded by the North Koreans who also use Ch'ongjin as a distributing center for the east coast.

WONSAN | Wonsan, on the Sea of Japan south of Hungnam, is one of North Korea's principal ports and a major naval base.

Fish are plentiful in the waters off Wonsan because of the presence of both a warm and a cold ocean current. The city's fine natural harbor is home port for many busy fishing boats whose catch includes pollack, octopus, sardines, herring, and mackerel.

Some of Wonsan's 215,000 residents work in fish processing plants. The city also has a large oil refinery, locomotive works, brickyards, and a ceramics industry. It is an important terminal for one of North Korea's railway networks.

Like many other Korean cities, Wonsan was partially destroyed during the Korean War. Since the war, its industries have been revived and expanded. The single-story houses and business establishments that once lined its streets have been replaced with blocks of multi-story apartment houses and office buildings.

20

P'ANMUNJOM

To Koreans, P'anmunjom serves as a reminder that peace has not yet returned to their country. P'anmunjom is located in the demilitarized zone that separates the Democratic People's Republic of Korea and the Republic of Korea. It was here that United Nations and Communist representatives met to work out the terms of the armistice that was signed on July 27, 1953. However, all attempts to replace the armistice with a peace treaty have failed and a state of war continues to exist between the two sides that fought the Korean War.

Negotiators representing North Korea and the United Nations meet in P'anmunjom's Military Armistice Commission building to deal with violations and other problems arising from the armistice. The building sits exactly astride the military demarcation line that separates the two Koreas.

The two sides share in the administration of the 151-mile-long buffer zone between the north and the south. Each is allowed 1,000 military policemen for patrol duty. United States soldiers who are assigned to the United Nations Command take part in the patrols. From time to time, gunfire has been exchanged by the patrols and raiders have managed to slip across the buffer zone. Aircraft belonging to one side or the other have been shot from the skies and ships have been captured in the waters off Korea. But the armistice agreement has remained in effect — the longest such agreement in history.

Above, delegates to the United Nations Commission
photograph the Freedom House near the Demilitarized Zone (DMZ)
at P'anmunjom, Korea. Left, a DMZ military policeman
stands guard at the southern boundary of the Zone, a checkpoint
manned by military personnel of the Republic of Korea Army.

21

REUNIFICATION
FOR KOREA

Ever since their country was divided at the 38th parallel at the end of World War II, the Korean people have hoped that the north and the south would one day be reunited. However, North Korea has been unwilling to give up its Communist government and South Korea has continued to be anti-Communist. Moreover, each has remained heavily armed and the two governments have bitterly criticized one another.

In spite of the seemingly irreconcilable differences between them, North and South Korea have begun to move closer together. At the suggestion of the Republic of Korea's Red Cross, talks aimed at re-uniting families separated by the Korean War got underway in 1971. The talks, held at P'anmunjom, Seoul, and Pyongyang, were the first peaceful contacts between the two Koreas in a quarter of a century.

When the talks began, no one expected the negotiations to move quickly or smoothly. But all Koreans hoped that they would lead to further contacts and to the eventual reunification of their country.

In spite of their differences, both North and South Koreans
are reminded of the Korean conflict by such grim scenes as this.
Here, graves of Turkish troops are marked with a star and crescent
at a United Nations cemetery.

INDEX

ABOUT THE AUTHORS

Colonel Gene Gurney, a U.S. Air Force specialist with many books to his credit, often teams with his wife, Clare, a former librarian. For Franklin Watts, Inc., they have co-authored such books as *Monticello*, *Mount Vernon*, and *FDR and Hyde Park*. The Gurneys make their home at Dares Beach, Maryland. Both Colonel Gurney and his wife have spent many months in Korea on Air Force tours of duty.